SERVING YOUR COUNTRY

THE UNITED STATES NAVY

by Michael Green

Content Consultant:

Jack A. Green, Historian
Naval Historical Center

C A P S T O N E
H I G H / L O W   B O O K S
an imprint of Capstone Press

C A P S T O N E P R E S S

818 North Willow Street • Mankato, Minnesota 56001
http://www.capstone-press.com

Library of Congress Cataloging-in-Publication Data
Green, Michael, 1952-
The United States Navy/by Michael Green.
    p. cm. -- (Serving your country)
    Includes bibliographical references and index.
    Summary: An introduction to the history, function, ships, and future of
the United States Navy.
    ISBN 1-56065-690-5
    1. United States. Navy--Juvenile literature. [1. United States. Navy.]
I. Title. II. Series.
VA55.G74 1998
359'.00973--dc21

                                                        97-35554
                                                          CIP
                                                          AC

Editorial credits:
Editor, Matt Doeden; cover design, Timothy Halldin; illustrations,
    James Franklin; photo research, Michelle L. Norstad
Photo credits:
Archive Photos, 43
Department of Defense, 15, 20, 22, 29
Michael Green, 5, 8, 11, 12, 24, 27, 30, 37
U.S. Navy/Felix Garza Jr.,cover, 34; "Bud" Warfield, 16; Joe Hendricks;
    18; John K. Sokolowski, 39; Robbie E. Russell, 32

Table of Contents

Chapter 1

The United States Navy

The United States Navy is one of the armed forces of the U.S. military. The navy uses warships and aircraft to protect the United States from attack. The navy patrols oceans to make sure no enemies are preparing to attack.

Officers and Enlisted Members

There are two main groups of people in the navy. They are officers and enlisted members. Both men and women can be officers or enlisted members. Officers have higher grades than enlisted members. Enlisted members must obey the orders of officers.

About 400,000 people serve in the U.S. Navy. About 60,000 of them are officers. The highest-ranking member of the navy is the

The U.S. Navy uses warships to protect the United States from attack.

chief of naval operations. The chief of naval operations runs the navy and makes sure it is ready for battle.

Officers and enlisted members each serve a service commitment. A service commitment is a set amount of service time. Service commitments last between four and eight years.

U.S. Navy Bases

Most people in the navy work on ships or at naval bases. Most naval bases have shipyards. A shipyard is a place where ships are built or repaired. Naval bases also have supply centers. Supply centers make sure ships have fuel, food, and weapons. Some bases have schools where instructors train members of the navy.

Many naval bases have air strips and hangars. An air strip is a smooth surface where airplanes take off and land. A hangar is a building used to store aircraft.

Operating Forces

Naval ships and their crews are called operating forces. Ships in the operating forces

IMPORTANT U.S. NAVY BASES

1) Everett, WA
2) San Diego, CA
3) Corpus Christi Air Station, TX
4) Pensacola Air Station, FL
5) Mayport, FL
6) Norfolk, VA
7) U.S. Naval Academy, MD
8) Great Lakes Training Center, IL
9) Pearl Harbor, HI

work together in fleets. A fleet is a group of warships under one command.

Navy members on a ship work together to keep the ship ready for battle. They often work with members of the U.S. Marine Corps. The Marine Corps does not have its own ships. During wartime, navy ships carry marines to battle sites. Navy ships often carry Marine Corps airplanes, too.

Chapter 2
History

The U.S. Navy became part of the U.S. military during the Revolutionary War (1775-1783). Members of the British colonies in America wanted to be free from Great Britain. The colonists started the Revolutionary War to win their freedom. They began building a navy to fight the British in 1775. The colonists called their navy the Continental navy.

At first, the Continental navy had no warships. Colonists turned cargo ships into warships. Cargo ships carry goods like food. The navy put guns on the cargo ships. The navy also added large sails that made the ships travel faster. The Continental navy used these ships to capture British ships. Often the British ships

The *Constitution* was one of the navy's first warships.

carried weapons. The Continental navy used these weapons against the British.

The U.S. government sold many of the Continental navy's ships after the end of the Revolutionary War. The government stopped spending money on the Continental navy. The government created the U.S. Navy in 1787.

Growth of the U.S. Navy

In 1845, the U.S. Navy formed a school in Annapolis, Maryland. The school became known as the U.S. Naval Academy. The navy began training its officers at the school.

Eleven Southern states seceded from the United States in 1861. Secede means to break away from a group. The states formed a new country called the Confederate States of America. This started the Civil War (1861-1865).

The U.S. Navy blockaded the Confederacy during the Civil War. Blockade means to prevent ships from delivering goods. The navy's blockade kept the Confederacy from receiving food and weapons. It helped the Northern states win the Civil War.

The navy formed the U.S. Naval Academy to train officers.

The navy built steel warships after the Civil War.

The navy began building stronger ships after the Civil War. The navy built steel ships. All the navy's ships were wooden before the Civil War.

In 1907, President Theodore Roosevelt wanted to show the world that the U.S. Navy was powerful. The navy painted its entire fleet white. The navy called it the Great White Fleet. Roosevelt sent the fleet around the world.

World Wars

The German navy used submarines during World War I (1914-1918). A submarine is a warship that can run on the surface of the water or underwater. The U.S. Navy had built only a few submarines at that time. None of them had worked well. The German navy's submarines were very successful. They sank many French and British ships. U.S. leaders decided to build more submarines after World War I.

The Japanese military bombed Pearl Harbor Naval Base, Hawaii, in 1941. This brought the United States into World War II (1939-1945). The United States used a large Pacific fleet during World War II. The fleet fought against the Japanese military on the Pacific Ocean. The navy also helped U.S. troops battle Germany in Europe.

The navy's Pacific fleet included submarines, aircraft carriers, and other kinds of ships. An aircraft carrier is a large warship that carries airplanes. Airplanes take off from and land on aircraft carriers. Powerful U.S. airplanes helped the United States and its allies win World War II. Allies are countries that work together. Many of these airplanes belonged to the navy.

After the World Wars

After World War II, the navy built better, faster aircraft. Aircraft carriers became more important. The navy also built better submarines.

Nuclear engines powered some submarines. Nuclear power is a kind of energy that lasts longer than other kinds of energy. Nuclear submarines can dive deeper than other submarines. Their engines are more powerful. They can also stay underwater longer because they do not have to refuel.

The U.S. Navy fought in the Korean War (1950-1953) and the Vietnam War (1954-1975). U.S. Navy ships brought marines to battles. Aircraft carriers carried aircraft used in the wars.

The navy helped the United States defeat Iraq during the Gulf War (1991). Aircraft with missiles took off from aircraft carriers during the war. A missile is an explosive that can travel long distances.

The Navy built better submarines after World War II.

Chapter 3
Navy Jobs

There are many jobs in the navy. Every member of the navy performs a certain job. The navy can defend the United States only if all of its members do their jobs.

Pilots

Pilots fly naval aircraft. They fly helicopters and fighter planes. They often take off from and land on aircraft carriers. U.S. Navy pilots fly patrol missions. A mission is a military task. On patrol missions, pilots look for enemy ships and aircraft.

Pilots also fly rescue missions. They often use helicopters for rescue missions. Some pilots fly attack missions. Pilots on attack

Pilots fly naval aircraft.

missions may bomb enemy sites or shoot enemy aircraft.

Pilots know how to use the weapons, instruments, and radios in their aircraft. They use guns and missiles to destroy enemy ships, aircraft, and sites. Pilots use instruments to establish where they are while flying. They use radios to talk to other members of the navy on ships and in other aircraft.

Intelligence Officers

Naval intelligence officers gather information about other countries' navies. They study new ships and aircraft that other countries are building. They help naval leaders decide what kinds of weapons the navy will need in the future.

During wartime, enemies may send messages in code. Some intelligence officers try to break these codes. Sometimes breaking codes helps the navy learn the enemies' plans.

Intelligence officers help navy leaders decide what kinds of weapons the navy will need in the future.

Gunner's mates know how to aim and fire naval guns.

Gunner's Mates

Gunner's mates repair naval guns and missiles. They test and inspect bullets and missiles. Gunner's mates make sure all the parts of guns and missiles are working.

During wartime, gunner's mates operate guns and missiles. They know how to aim and fire guns at enemy aircraft and warships. They must be able to fix a gun or missile quickly if it stops working.

Mechanics

Mechanics keep naval engines working. Some naval mechanics fix the large engines in ships. Others fix aircraft engines.

Some mechanics work on ground crews. Ground crews help aircraft take off from the ground and from aircraft carriers. Mechanics on ground crews check engines to make sure they are working properly. They check oil pressure and temperature. Mechanics ground aircraft if there are problems with the engines. Ground means to keep from flying.

Navigator

Navigators navigate ships. Navigate means to steer or guide. Navigators always know where their ships are in the ocean. They also track other nearby ships. Navigators must know whether the other ships are U.S. Navy ships.

Navigators know how to read naval maps and charts. They use maps and charts to guide ships

away from land and shallow waters. They also know how to use radar. Radar is machinery that uses radio waves to locate and guide objects.

Navy SEALs

The Navy SEALs is a specially trained combat group within the navy. SEAL stands for Sea, Air, and Land. SEALs must know how to fight in all of these places. They must be strong swimmers. They also must be able to jump out of airplanes and fight on land.

During wartime, SEALs secretly attack enemies. They move in the water without being detected. Sometimes they move in boats. Other times they walk or swim through shallow water.

Navy SEALs must be in excellent shape. They must be able to endure danger and rough conditions. They must be strong and they must be able to fight well. Only the best members of the navy become SEALs.

Navy SEALs must be able to fight well.

Chapter 4

Ships and Aircraft

The U.S. Navy uses warships and aircraft to defend the United States. Naval fleets include aircraft carriers, submarines, cruisers, and other small ships. Cruisers protect aircraft carriers. Submarines attack enemy ships and protect aircraft carriers.

Aircraft Carriers

Aircraft carriers are so large that they look like floating air strips. Aircraft carriers carry many kinds of aircraft, including fighter planes and helicopters. Aircraft carriers also carry ground crews and radar equipment.

The *Harry S. Truman* is the U.S. Navy's largest aircraft carrier. It is 1,096 feet

Aircraft carriers carry many aircraft.

(329 meters) long. This is as long as the Empire State Building is tall. The *Harry S. Truman* can carry a crew of about 5,500 people. It also can carry about 90 aircraft.

Submarines

Submarines are difficult for people to spot from the surface of the ocean. This is because they spend most of their time underwater. Traveling underwater allows submarines to move close to enemy ships and attack them.

One of the navy's newest submarines is the *Seawolf*. The *Seawolf* cost more than $2 billion to build. It is 353 feet (108 meters) long. It can carry a crew of 134 people. The *Seawolf* can travel at speeds up to 28 miles (45 kilometers) per hour. Its weapons include missiles and torpedoes. Torpedoes are explosives that can travel underwater.

Cruisers

Cruisers are medium-sized warships. They are fast. Some travel up to 35 miles (56 kilometers) per hour. They have powerful guns, missiles, and

The newest U.S. Navy cruiser is the *Ticonderoga*.

torpedoes. Cruisers protect aircraft carriers. They also attack enemy ships and objects on land.

The newest navy cruiser is the *Ticonderoga*. The *Ticonderoga* has advanced weapons systems. It carries large missiles and guns. It also carries a helicopter. The helicopter can attack enemy submarines and fly patrol missions. The *Ticonderoga* can carry a crew of more than 350 people.

Fighter Planes

Naval fighter planes attack enemy ships and aircraft. They also protect naval planes, aircraft carriers, and other naval ships. Naval fighter planes have powerful weapons. They carry guns and missiles. Some carry bombs.

The F/14 Tomcat is the navy's fastest fighter. It can fly more than 1,750 miles (2,818 kilometers) per hour. Another naval fighter is the F/A-18 Hornet. The Hornet is smaller than the Tomcat. It cannot fly as fast as the Tomcat. But it turns and dives more quickly than the Tomcat. This allows Hornet pilots to act quickly if an enemy attacks.

Helicopters

The navy uses helicopters to scout for enemy fleets. Some helicopters have special weapons that can destroy enemy submarines. Other helicopters carry people and supplies from one ship to another.

Pilots use naval fighter planes to attack enemy ships and aircraft.

The SH-3H Sea King has special equipment that helps pilots detect enemy submarines. This helicopter also carries torpedoes that pilots can drop on enemy submarines. Sea King pilots often fly patrol missions.

A-7E CORSAIR II FIGHTER PLANES

RADAR

BRIDGE

USS NIMITZ AIRCRAFT CARRIER

FLIGHT DECK

ELEVATOR

HULL

Chapter 5
Training

Members of the U.S. Navy receive special training. They learn in classes and take tests. Naval officers receive more training than enlisted members. Officers also must graduate from college.

Enlisted Member Training

Enlisted members begin their naval careers in basic training. They are called seamen recruits while they are in basic training. Seaman recruit is the lowest grade in the navy.

All seamen recruits attend basic training at the Great Lakes Training Center in northern Illinois. They form groups of 80 people. Each group is called a ship. Members of each ship go through drills and tests together. They also take classes together.

Members of the U.S. Navy receive special training.

Enlisted members begin their careers as seamen recruits.

The navy promotes seamen recruits who finish basic training to seamen apprentices. Promote means to give a higher grade. Seamen apprentices receive more training after basic training. They learn about naval jobs. Some may learn about becoming mechanics. Others might learn about becoming gunner's mates.

The highest grade an enlisted member can earn is master chief petty officer. Master chief petty officers work with officers and enlisted members. They help enlisted members carry out officers' orders. They also tell officers when other enlisted members have questions or complaints.

Enlisted members also can become officers. They must earn college degrees and receive extra training.

Officer Training

Naval officers receive special training that enlisted members do not receive. Officers receive this training in one of three ways. They may train at the U.S. Naval Academy. They may attend Officers Candidate School. Or they may take part in a Reserve Officers Training Corps (ROTC) program. An ROTC program teaches its members military leadership skills while they attend college.

The U.S. Naval Academy is in Annapolis, Maryland. People who train at the Naval Academy are called midshipmen. Both men and women can train at the Naval Academy.

Midshipmen learn about the navy and about different jobs. They learn about leadership. They also take regular classes like math and history. Midshipmen receive college degrees when they graduate. A college degree is a title given to a person for completing a course of study.

College graduates can become naval officers by completing Officers Candidate School. Officers Candidate School lasts 13 weeks. Members become officers when they complete the school.

Some officers receive training through ROTC programs. The navy's ROTC program prepares college students to become naval officers. Students attend classes about the navy as well as regular college classes.

Midshipmen train at the U.S. Naval Academy.

Naval officers start with the grade of ensign. Ensign is the lowest grade an officer can have. Admiral is the highest grade an officer can earn.

Navy Reserves

Some officers and enlisted members join the U.S. Navy Reserves. Members of the reserves are not on active duty. Active duty is full-time military work. Reserve members attend training once a month. They also serve the navy for two full weeks each year. The navy may place its reserves on active duty if it needs more people.

Officers and enlisted members in the Navy Reserves receive the same training as people on active duty. Many members of the Navy Reserves are people who have finished service commitments. Some are people who work for the navy but also have other jobs.

Admiral is the highest grade an officer can earn.

Chapter 6
The Future

Today, some U.S. leaders believe there is little chance of major wars. They believe there is no need for a large U.S. Navy. As a result, the government has cut some of the navy's funding.

The U.S. Navy has become smaller because of these cuts. But the navy is still strong. It continues to develop stronger and less expensive equipment to defend the United States. This equipment includes new ships and aircraft.

New Warships

The U.S. Navy recently has built new warships like the *Seawolf* and the *Harry S. Truman*. The navy now plans to build new warships. Navy leaders hope these warships will be better and less expensive than today's warships.

The *Seawolf* is one of the navy's newest warships.

New Aircraft

Aircraft play an important role in modern combat. The U.S. Navy is building new and better aircraft to defend the United States and its allies.

The Joint Advanced Strike Technology (JAST) program is building new kinds of aircraft for the navy. The JAST program is building aircraft that can take off from special ramps on aircraft carriers. The navy will be able to launch these aircraft quickly.

New aircraft and warships will help the U.S. Navy remain powerful in the future. The new equipment will help the navy keep the United States safe.

The navy plans to build new and better warships.

WORDS TO KNOW

air strip (AIR STRIP)—a smooth surface where airplanes take off and land

aircraft carrier (AIR-kraft KAIR-ee-ur)—a large warship that carries airplanes

blockade (blok-ADE)—to prevent ships from delivering goods

fleet (FLEET)—a group of warships under one command

hangar (HANG-ur)—a building used to store aircraft

mission (MISH-uhn)—a military task

promote (pruh-MOTE)—to give a higher grade

radar (RAY-dar)—machinery that uses radio waves to locate and guide objects

shipyard (SHIP-yard)—a place where ships are built or repaired

submarine (SUHB-muh-reen)—a warship that can run on the surface of the water or underwater

TO LEARN MORE

Black, Wallace B. *Blockade Runners and Ironclads: Naval Action in the Civil War.* New York: Franklin Watts, 1997.

Green, Michael. *The United States Marines.* Mankato, Minn: Capstone High/Low Books, 1998.

Hole, Dorothy. *The Navy and You.* New York: Crestwood House, 1993.

Streissguth, Thomas. *U.S. Navy SEALs.* Minneapolis: Capstone Press, 1996.

USEFUL ADDRESSES

Intrepid Sea-Air-Space Museum
Pier 86
West 46th Street and 12th Avenue
New York, NY 10036

Naval Historical Center
Washington Navy Yard
901 M Street SE
Washington, DC 20374-5060

Submarine Memorial Museum
P.O. Box 395
Hackensack, NJ 07602

USS Lexington Museum
2914 North Shoreline Boulevard
Corpus Christi, TX 78403-3076

INTERNET SITES

The Big Mamie Home Page
http://www.ici.net/cust_pages/jack/mamie.html

U.S. Navy History
http://www.history.navy.mil

United States Naval & Shipbuilding Museum Online
http://www.uss-salem.org/

U.S. Navy: Welcome Aboard
http://www.navy.mil/

USS Kitty Hawk
http://trout.nosc.mil/~cv63pao/

INDEX